Finding Peace

Patricia Hellriegel

BookLeaf
Publishing

India | USA | UK

Presentation by *BookLeaf Publishing*

Web: www.bookleafpub.com

E-mail: info@bookleafpub.com

ISBN: 9789357446525

First edition 2022

DEDICATION

To my university, for never giving up on me
and continuing to grow my mind. Thank you!

ACKNOWLEDGE MENT

From the bottom of my heart, I thank you for picking up this little book of mine. It really means a lot to me. Hopefully, you have found some hope and peace from it, too. Your "finding peace" journey may look completely different, but that is okay. God is there for you, too.

Thank you so much to BookLeaf Publishing and their 21 Days Writing Challenge. It is what I needed to take my poetic finding peace journey to the next level and to share my story. It was a remarkable journey to put these poems in the order they are, and also to write them.

Additionally, thank you to everyone who, knowingly or unknowingly, played a big or small part in the life story that has made me the me I am today. I couldn't have done it without you. And I, especially, want to thank my family, for being the pillars in my life.

I also want to say thank you to my amazing university, for providing me with the time and resources to discover the me I want to be, and helping me find ways as to how I can make it a reality. I wouldn't have reached the level of understanding without my not quite finished university years.

I also want to thank everyone who has ever wronged or hurt me in the past, for it has shaped me, too. Yet, it will only ever be worth mentioning as a footnote in my life's story, as there are more important things about me.

Last, but definitely not least, I thank Jesus, for He is my ultimate protector and provider of strength, peace, and love.

PREFACE

I never knew that poetry,
would be part of my story.

But if this is my way
to bring You glory,
I am okay
to share my story,
which is really Yours for sure anyways, sorry.

It's like my thoughts fly out,
that never found my mouth.

Thoughts that know about me,
what I cannot see.

Thoughts that feel,
what I have tried to seal.

My thoughts are put into words,
which no longer feel like swords,
but rather like save forts.

It Started by Drowning

I have been drowning in my past,
time has been running so fast.
It's like I just started at my dream school,
not knowing the plans to make me a fool.

I trusted you, dear friend.
Though, nothing can mend
what you have done,
for my old me is gone.

You left me drowning even in the middle of
masses.
As a result, I was failing all my classes.
Admit it, you never cared,
just were proud for another victim to have been
lured.

Well, guess what?
I am over that!
You wanted to break me,
I am stronger now, don't you see?

All your destructions,
fit right into God's construction.
For what you tried to destroy,
God plans to apply,
so a new better me is able to be put into this
reality.

You had your chance,
yet not alone I am going to dance
because you had your plan,
but a way better one my God can.

You had me drowning in my past,
well, thank you, I'll be free at last!

A Me to Be

I am not me!
Cannot I see?

Whenever a guy shows any interest in me,
it seems that I lose the key,
to the real me.

I try so hard to please,
that I start to cease.
I try so hard to be loved,
that I get cuffed.

I just want to be me,
you'll see.

Who am I?
When everything I do feels like a flawed reality?

I am not me when I am with you.
So, I think I have to go.
I have to stop the show,

maybe even lay low.

All I know is that it has to be now.

I may not know who I am,
but I can.
I'll figure out the real me,
and make everyone see,
who I'll be.

A me to rise,
and a me to choose wise.
A me to hear,
and a me to bear.

I will not back down,
from the life that was shown.

Realization

Now it seems clear,
the reason why I'm here.

It's by knowing myself,
and not just sitting on a shelf,
that I know about You,
and learn to love You, too.

Everything I think, speak and do,
should bring me and others to You.

How can I become
with you one?

You are my Lord,
You lay out the accord.
You are my Savior,
able to erase all my failure.
You are God,
I love You a lot!

Choice

I don't have to choose,
which church community to lose.

For You have put me here,
Your intentions have always been clear.

For You have put me there,
to learn more about You to share.

I know now that I can serve You everywhere.

You know where I need to be,
and what I chase
for people to see.
Your grace,
you gifted me.

I don't want to disappoint You,
for I love You, too.

So, here is what I choose:
It will always be You.

Trust

There is freedom
in Your kingdom.

Jesus Christ,
You're the only one to make us rise.
You give us peace
because it's through You that we'll release.
You love us,
even though we get lost in world's lust.
You died,
to make things right.

I am sorry for all the pain I've caused,
and for feeling like I'm a lost cause.
It was never about me.
Now, I can see.

This life I live,
You were the one to give.
I am here because of You,
to help others see You, too.

I am not quite sure how yet,
but You'll show it to me, I bet.
I trust You,
for You know exactly what to do.

My life is in Your hands.
I know that now I have a chance,
to dance,
and maybe finally find my own romance.

But You know what I need,
so it's You that I seek,
and Your every word to feed.

The Real Me

It's like I've been a puppet on strings,
letting others decide on life things.
I've been other people's me,
acting out what they wanted to see.

You should stop and read,
what I put down on these sheets.

I am not your doll,
nor your punching bag for your groll.

I am me,
wearing jeans and a tee,
or going full glam,
living as being part of fashion's
cream-de-la-cream.

I love snuggling up
with a tea cup.
I am a book, music, TV show dork,
and am also a believer in our Heavenly Lord.

Time to Be Thine

Don't have energy anymore,
feeling like drifting off-shore.

I am just so tired,
with my head being out-wired.

Just need time for myself,
picking up a book from its shelf,
and starting to read,
or letting myself fall into the sheets,
not thinking who when to meet,
but simply to keep
me in Your presence,
finishing up this sentence.

My batteries are charging,
but yet not quite enlarging.

I need time,
time to be truly Thine.

Seeking Purpose

My depression cannot be cured,
it will always be the one to lure.
Instead the least I can hope for is to be in
remission.
A way that keeps me on track with Your
mission.

Being back here,
makes darkness feel so near.

I need Your help.
I need to know how it has felt.
The life that was filled with laughter.
I need to know there is an after.

Please, help me see,
a different version of me.

Please, help me be,
for Your kingdom a key.

Hope

I had another nightmare.
Sometimes I just wish I would not care.
It would make life easier,
without these dreams as a teaser.

I want to let go of all things scaring me.
Yet, I cannot stop to see,
what was done to me.

Waiting for when Your Love overcomes,
making the pain I feel only some.

Some pain from my past,
something that doesn't last
because You are greater.
You help me feel lighter.

I could use one of Your miracles again.
Something to keep me sane.

Maybe

Maybe it's time to stop
caring to always talk shop.

Maybe it's time to see
depression as a part of me.

Maybe it is not as evil as I want it to be.
Maybe I should get another cup of tea,
gaining me strength.

Hence,
my depression can be a good thing,
for whenever I feel tingling,
I know I should be thinking,
how I was made loving
to be a cause for Your workings.

Presence

Sitting here
near water
depression getting shorter.

The sun shining on my face,
seeing a bit clearer Your case.

Oh, how I enjoy this peace
feeling my depression to finally cease.

Listening to my old playlist,
I lived with when my life was still stuck in a
mist.

Now, each song
is what for I long.

Please Help Me

Working to get into a productive schedule,
one that doesn't lull.

Now, that I am alive,
I am ready to dive
right in,
leaving behind all my sin.

I hope You forgive me,
for me to have spilled my cup of tea,
when it never should have been about me.
Now, I can see.

It's You.
I love You, too.
I let You decide,
on which side of life I should reside.

But please forgive me,
for not seeing sooner,
that You are the one and only trooper.

You are the creator of Heaven and Earth.
You have control over me and my nerves.

My thoughts are Yours.
Please give me strength to keep them on tour.

Help me not lose sight,
of what is right.

Help me to stay true,
to the real me planned by You.

I want to see You,
and love You, too.

Please keep me in You,
as without You I cannot live, too.

Prayer

Your Word I am reading.
My Soul is bleeding.

It hit me so hard.
I could fall apart.

I am broken.
Nobody's token.

I need You to be near.
My sight to be made sheer.

I need You here.
So I will not tear.

Please, don't give up on me,
but help me see,
the remarkable Love of Thee.

Be Worthy

The night is dark.
I am caught by a shark.

Depression has me pushed back in
the deep and ugly pit of sin.

What do I do wrong?
I thought it's only true love I long?

I don't know what to do.
I could use Your cue.

I don't know where to go,
other than that I don't want to be low.

Please help me see
a way to be
like someone worth deserving Thee.

Life

Life.
It's like taking a deep dive.

It's getting dark,
and you're getting hunted by more than one
shark,
and then it gets even darker,
the knives in your back are made sharper.

And when all strength has left you,
there is only one more thing to do:

Fall down on to your knees,
and simply be.
Here in the presence of the Lord,
you'll find true comfort.

With Him you come up to the surface,
as He is giving you true purpose.

Jesus, You are

Learned today about the husband-tree.
Now I kind of see.

As an example they gave the grapevine tree,
immediately I thought of Thee.

I am Yours,
for sure.

How would I ever find a Liam Rys or Jack
Thornton?
Life isn't a wishing fountain.

Jesus,
You are enough.
You make me laugh.
You are great.
You are who helped me get made.
You are love.
You bring us peace through a dove.

Change

I feel changed,
like my thoughts got rearranged.

I feel the worth,
like again I am allowed to call it my turf.

Thank You for never leaving me,
and letting me be.

It may took way too long a time,
but it was needed to find the words for this
rhyme.

I don't know if I can ever thank You enough,
but I try by gifting You my love.

A Good Life

And suddenly I really see,
that moment when my life started to cease.
The big change in my life,
was when it was over with US5.

I still miss my boys,
have they brought me so much joy.
They will always stay in my heart,
for they have played such a vital part.

I wouldn't be me,
without the four boys plus Richie.
I wouldn't know what love is,
or how it feels to truly miss.

They are such a big part of my life's story,
with moments for which I will never be sorry.
I miss them.
My love for them still being the same.

Thank You for making me realize,

that my life was and is so nice.
I feel truly whole again,
finally being in the right lane.

I love You,
thank You for guiding me through.
I will never let You go,
always letting You make me more grow.

I am no longer in a cave,
for You have me saved.
You are the only one in life I need,
to succeed.

No More

Falling right back in,
feeling like a sardine in a tin.
Trapped in other people's decisions,
ignoring my mission.

I need to find a way,
away.

I want to live out my talents,
starting to pay amends,
and all my doubts finally to the trash send.

I feel like my voice was stolen.
I am not just a pretty token.

My voice needs to be heard,
and my thoughts need to be shared.

I am not in hiding anymore.
I won't back down, for sure!

At Church

Decided to get back into journaling,
as written words are more my thing.
It's how I express myself.
It's how I bring order to all the thoughts on my
shelf.

Back at church again,
celebrating Your reign.
Being able to sit with a view at the picture of
You,
the one that helped me through.

Through all of the past year,
providing a way for me to still be here.
I love this place.
It's like I can really sense Your grace.

Thank You for everything,
You truly are our King.

Peace at Last

I just read through all my poems,
capturing all my last year´s moments.

I survived a lot.
I still have left a shot.

My life isn't over.
There is going to be another October.

I will never give up,
but grabbing a filled tea cup,
and look up to You
because You make things true.

Thank You,
I love You, too.